STOCK CAR RACING

Bill Holder

Photography by Bob Fairman

Foreword by Dick Berggren

Editor, *Stock Car Racing* Magazine; Stock Car Racing Commentator, ESPN Television

GALLERY BOOKS
An imprint of W.H. Smith Publishers Inc.
112 Madison Avenue
New York, New York 10016

OLDS
DEERY BROS. OLDS
Cedar Falls, Ia.
SCOOTER'S
Kathie
76
DieHard
Stewart
MOROSO
Edelbrock
MAC TOOLS
VICTOR
WISECO
OLDSMOBILE

STOCK CAR RACING

Contents

Foreword   9
History   10
The Tracks   14
The Crew   20
The Cars   34
Behind the Wheel   46
Index   80

Published by Gallery Books
A Division of W H Smith Publishers Inc.
112 Madison Avenue
New York, New York 10016

Produced by
Brompton Books Corp.
15 Sherwood Place
Greenwich, CT 06830

ISBN 0-8317-6301-9

Printed in Hong Kong

10 9 8 7 6 5 4 3 2 1

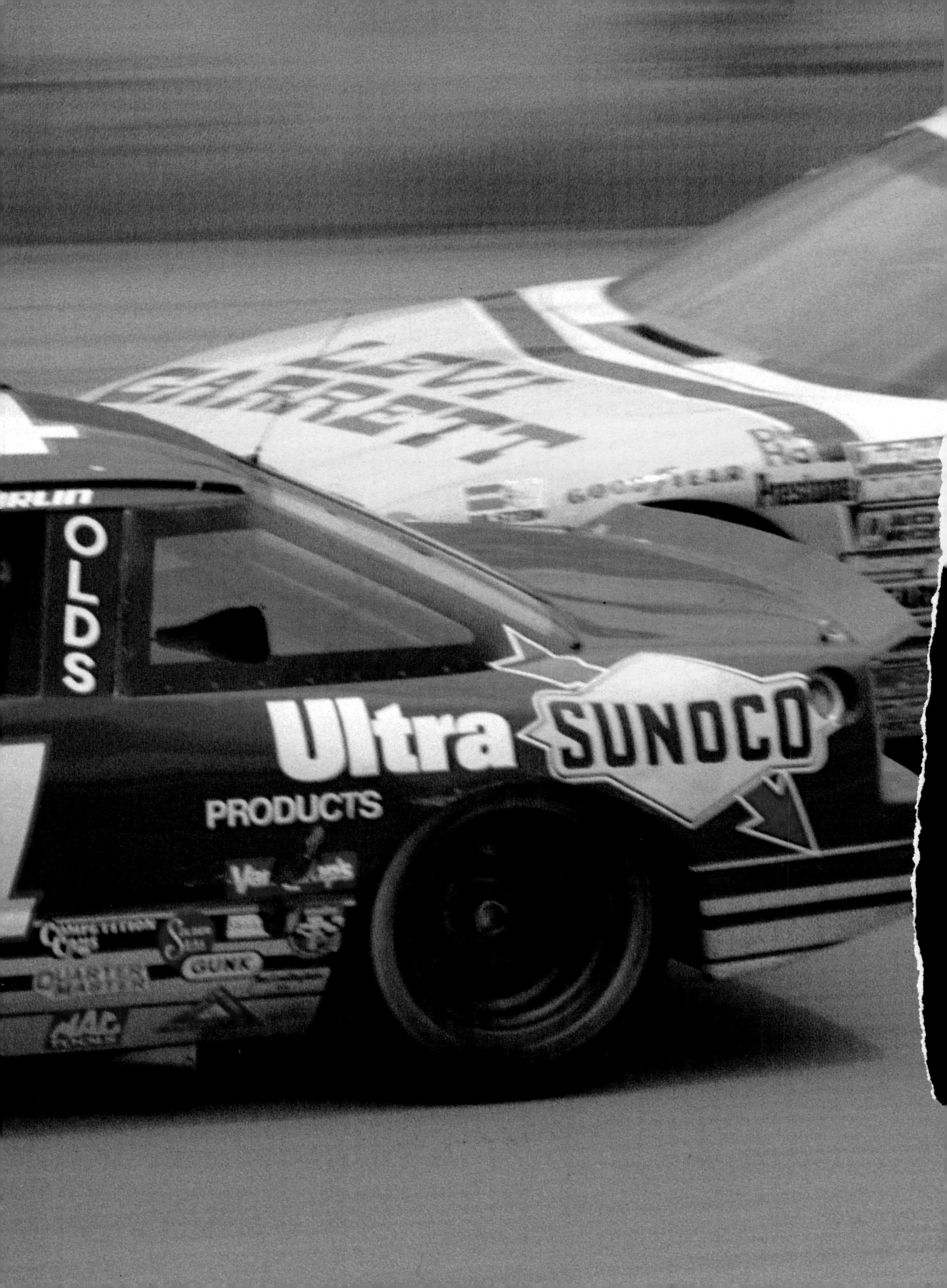
OLDS
Ultra
SUNOCO
PRODUCTS
GUNK

This book is dedicated to those brave warriors who put their lives, hearts and souls on the line every time they strap themselves into their stock cars and go to battle for the checkered flag.

Acknowledgments

The following tracks have provided valuable assistance and cooperation for this book:

Eldora Speedway, Rossburg, Ohio
Columbus Motor Speedway, Columbus, Ohio
Louisville Motor Speedway, Louisville, Kentucky
Daytona International Speedway, Daytona Beach, Florida
Bristol International Speedway, Bristol, Tennessee
Dover Downs International Speedway, Dover, Delaware
Kil-Kare Speedway, Xenia, Ohio
Talladega International Speedway, Talladga, Alabama
Martinsville Speedway, Martinsville, Virginia
Winchester Speedway, Winchester, Indiana
Shady Bowl Speedway, DeGraff, Ohio

The author and photographer would like to thank their wives, Ruthann Holder and Mary Fairman, without whose support and encouragement this book would not have been possible.

The author and publisher would also like to thank the following people who helped with the preparation of this book: Adrian Hodgkins, the designer; Jean Martin, the editor; and Florence Norton, the indexer.

All photos in this book were taken by Bob Fairman, except for the following:
Alabama International Speedway: 14, 73.
Rick Battle: 3-6.
Daytona International Speedway: 13, 15, 69, 78.
John Farquhar: 19.
Bill Holder: 10.
David Tucker: 11, 12, 62, 66-7.

Foreword

Stock car racing began its current wave of popularity in the early 1950s, when midget race cars became too expensive and people began to realize just how dangerous they were. In the beginning, a driver could earn a little money while becoming a local hero behind the wheel of a stock car. More recently, Rusty Wallace, the 1989 champion in Winston Cup stock car racing (the sport's highest level) earned over $3 million in a single year while becoming a hero to millions who watched him in person and on television.

This is a sport of brave men who literally risk their lives as part of the competition. Courage can lead to success, but it can also lead to disaster. This is a sport where to lose can literally mean losing everything – including life itself. To win can mean winning everything: money, fame, and adulation. Few activities in modern life offer as stark a set of alternatives or as much challenge as this one.

Stock car racing is enjoying its finest hour as this book is published. Every big league stock car race is televised, most of them live. Corporate support now approaches $100 million per year nationwide, and crowd counts at races, like the horsepower engine builders produce each year, keep getting bigger with each passing season.

Although stock car racing is often perceived as a regionalized sport, with its base in the American South, in fact it takes place in every state in America except Rhode Island where, curiously, it is against the law.

Far more cars and drivers compete as a hobby at small quarter-mile, third-mile, and half-mile ovals on Saturday nights in the summer than are involved in big league racing. From the dirt tracks of Iowa to the lights of the fancy paved ovals in Florida, stock car racing is truly America's sport.

Dick Berggren
Editor, *Stock Car Racing* Magazine;
Stock Car Racing Commentator, ESPN Television

Page 1: *Bill Elliott (9) and Alan Kulwicki (7) lead the pack on a restart in a NASCAR Winston Cup race at the Martinsville Speedway.*

The sport of stock car racing has come a long way in a very short time. Stock car racing really didn't start until the 1930s, and at that time, racing was a very amateur and primitive affair. Thanks to America's love affair with the automobile following World War II, when the country was tired of war and wanted to have a little fun, auto racing as a sport really took off.

Racing pioneer Bill France Sr. saw the great potential of the sport, and formed the now-famous National Association for Stock Car Racing (NASCAR), with the first race taking place under his direction in 1948. Four decades later, the prestigious sanctioning body is the king of the sport and is largely responsible for making auto racing one of the top spectator sports in the United States. Its stars – Richard Petty, Darrell Waltrip, Bill Elliott, Dale Earnhardt and others – are as well-known as any major league baseball player or NFL football performer. NASCAR races now enjoy national TV exposure along with heavy coverage in the printed media. Many of the biggest NASCAR races draw crowds well into the six-figure category.

NASCAR's key to success was, and still is today, the overall goal of keeping the competition on the track equal. Having eight or ten cars on the same lap with all of them having a chance to win is a tremendous crowd-pleaser and continues to bring out fans of big-time stock car racing in record numbers. The organization also established a number of safety rules which have been adopted by many other stock car racing organizations.

In the early days of stock car racing, NASCAR allowed only minor alterations to be made to the cars. For example, in 1949, a car was disqualified for racing with a non-factory angle iron. Later, the

Below: Ace stock car builder Ralph Moody started his racing career as a driver in vintage coupes such as this one. This type of racing served as a springboard to big-time racing. This restored early Ford was one of his successful cars.

organization would allow certain modifications to the cars that would make them more race cars than passenger cars. That trend has continued through the years. The car factories were not involved in those early days, and their involvement in later years would prove to have a great influence on the sport.

By the time the 1950s had arrived, NASCAR was running four dozen races a year. The races were mostly in the South, but Bill France was looking northward in hopes of making his race cars with fenders a national show. During the 1960s, that goal would be realized as NASCAR races would be run all over the country. NASCAR called its racing the Grand National series, a name it would retain into the 1980s. The name for that top-of-the-line series would then be changed to Winston Cup, in recognition of the series' national sponsor.

Left: *Richard Petty, the undisputed king of stock car racing in America. Now in the twilight of his career, Petty's 200 NASCAR victories probably will never be surpassed.*

Below: *NASCAR superstar Fred Lorenzen drove this Holman-Moody-built Ford to many victories during the mid-1960s. Oddly, Lorenzen retired at the height of his career.*

Above: *Once a highly successful driver, Junior Johnson is now an even more successful team owner, with several championships during the 1980s.*

Right: *In the late 1960s and early 1970s, Chrysler built its famous winged cars for NASCAR competition. Cars like this 1970 Dodge Daytona were quickly legislated out of competition and into collectors' hands.*

Later, NASCAR would broaden its influence with the introduction of several off-shoot series of cars. A very successful sportsman car series using smaller engines than the Grand National cars would serve as a proving ground for the top series. The series continues today and is called the Busch Grand National Series. Another series is the Winston West Series, held in the western United States. In the early years, NASCAR even had an open wheel division, although it didn't last.

Other organizations followed the NASCAR lead. In the 1950s, former driver John Marcum moved stock car racing up north and formed the Midwest Association of Race Cars (MARC), later renamed the Automobile Racing Club of America (ARCA). ARCA has run many joint shows with NASCAR, including the opening race at Daytona. The organization has served as a training ground for many NASCAR drivers, including Troy Ruttman, Freddy Lorenzen, Benny Parsons and Davey Allison.

During the 1970s, the interest in so-called "pony cars" promoted the formation of four new stock car bodies. The American Speed Association (ASA), All-Pro, American-Canadian Tour (ACT), and ARTGO organizations would specialize on the short tracks of the South and Midwest. Initially, all the circuits were dominated by Chevy Camaros and Pontiac Firebirds, but in recent years all body styles have been introduced.

The United States Auto Club (USAC) was also a very strong stock car body during the 1960s and 1970s. Many of its drivers would go on to excel in Indy car competition. Bobby and Al Unser, Mario Andretti and A J Foyt were but a few of the versatile racers who drove stock cars and Indy cars on the midwestern circuits. In fact, during the 1960s, the USAC compared quite well with NASCAR, and was even known in some quarters as the "NASCAR of the North."

These organizations deal primarily with pavement racing, and others are mainly concerned with dirt racing. A true racing fan will like one form of racing or the other, but never both. The most wide-reaching dirt stock car sanctioning body is UMP (United Midwestern Promoters), which ranks hundreds of dirt drivers nationwide on their performances at their local tracks. The STARS (Short Track Auto Racing Stars), All-Stars and PROS (Professional Racers Organization Series)

organizations are also very active in the eastern United States. More recently, the World of Outlaws sprint car organization formed a nationwide dirt stock car group in the 1980s.

A majority, though, of the stock car racing in this country, on both dirt and pavement, is done at the grass roots level on hundreds of hometown tracks, with local heroes doing the driving. That's the way it all began and is still the strength of the sport today. A few of these tracks run non-sanctioned spectaculars for huge purses. The most famous of these special events is the World 100 for dirt stock cars at Eldora Speedway in western Ohio. The event, which started in 1971, is the kingpin of the dirt stock car races. A win at the World is the ultimate goal for every dirt driver. Victory in 1989 was worth a cool $25,000.

Several other big dirt shows offer $50,000 or more to win, and such events draw the best cars in the nation to compete for not only the money, but also the prestige of winning. Just making the starting field in these super-competitive events is a major accomplishment, and winning is like a dream come true.

Born and raised in the United States, stock car racing is a purely American sport which has gone on to generate interest in other countries. The sport has become big business in the 1980s, and, as we enter the 1990s, you can be sure that the final plateau has yet to be reached.

Top: *Country and Western singer Marty Robbins was a frequent competitor in NASCAR competition during the 1970s. Here, Marty awaits his turn to qualify for the 1975 Daytona 500.*

Above: *The singer famous for "A White Sport Coat and a Pink Carnation" was a serious competitor on the NASCAR circuit when his show business obligations allowed.*

The Tracks

There has always been an unwritten rule that stock car racing is done on an oval-shaped track. It started out that way, and for the most part, has remained in that "left-turn only" format. The only deviation has been that NASCAR has run a limited number of road course races at locations such as Riverside, California and Watkins Glen, New York.

The initial tracks where stocks first ran, of course, were nothing more than carved-out clay ovals in backwoods cornfields. One of the earliest was the historic New Bremen, Ohio Speedway, built in 1926. It was started when a group of local farmers had visited the Indy 500 race and came back wanting a place to race their Model Ts. The flat-banked dirt track had races into the early 1980s before finally closing.

Many tracks sprang up after World War II, with the start of NASCAR activities. NASCAR's first national exposure came with its Labor Day race at

Right: *The 2.66-mile tri-oval with the turns banked at 33 degrees gives Talladega the distinction of being the world's fastest closed course race circuit. The tremendous speeds at Talladega during the late 1980s were partly responsible for a new ruling requiring carburetor restrictor plates to slow the cars down on superspeedway racetracks. Without the restrictor plates, speeds would easily exceed 220 miles per hour. Freight-train "drafting" is common at this track.*

the then brand-new Darlington, South Carolina Speedway in 1950. It was the first ever 500-mile race, and laid the groundwork for the NASCAR sport as it is known today. Over 100 cars were at that first event, with the winning car (hardly a high-performance racing machine – a six-cylinder Plymouth) the victor at only 76 miles per hour.

During the 1950s, NASCAR made headlines every February when its stock cars ran on the sand at Daytona Beach, Florida. It was a strange course, about four miles in length, with half of the racing surface being the beach itself and the other half being the highway that parallels the beach. Old-time drivers remember racing on the beach as one of their biggest thrills. The great race lasted until the late 1950s, when something even bigger came into the sport.

The new term in the business was "super-speedway." It started when Bill France decided to construct a two-and-a-half mile high-banked

Below: Ricky Rudd leads a ten-car pack through the Daytona International Speedway high banks. At 200 miles per hour, distances between the cars can sometimes be measured in inches. Touching another car at these speeds can be disastrous.

facility outside Daytona. The magnificent facility was capable of handling speeds of 170 miles per hour. Racing fans and drivers alike had never seen such speeds on a racing surface, and it vaulted NASCAR into the national limelight. The interest in this track caused construction to begin on similar tracks at Atlanta, Georgia, Charlotte, North Carolina and Talladega, Alabama. Also during that period, a number of mile and half-mile tracks were built.

Although only a few new speedways have been built recently, this is certainly no indication that the popularity of stock car racing has decreased. In fact, quite the opposite is true. Judging from attendance figures through the 1980s, the sport continues to grow at a steady rate, gaining new fans every year. There have been continuous improvements to the older tracks to keep them up with the times and the increased performance of

the racing machines. The Richmond, Virginia Speedway was actually lengthened from a half-mile to a three-quarter mile distance for the 1989 season.

A showplace for stock car short track racing in the 1990s is the brand-new Louisville Motor Speedway. It is the most high-tech short paved track racing facility in the nation. Built with the family in mind, the track features supervised play areas, a teenage video game room, deli-type food, VIP suites and a clown for the kids. And, of course, there is stock car racing on the track.

Quite apart from the world of pavement racing is the whole other world of dirt tracking. This is a world of hundreds of tiny dusty ovals sprinkled across the country. Many are fairground tracks that have been in place for many decades. Many of the tracks are tucked away deep in the country, accessible only by narrow two-lane roads.

Below left: *Sponsorship is an important part of both long and short track racing in America. Here, national racing sponsors show their colors at Indianapolis Raceway Park.*

Below: *The Columbus (Ohio) Motor Speedway is a very active short track in the Midwest. Here, the cars of the American Speed Association line up for driver introductions at the 1989 season-opening race. The slightly banked one-third-mile oval makes for tight door-to-door racing.*

Above: The Martinsville Speedway, with its long straightaways and tight turns, epitomizes NASCAR short track racing. All of the on-track and pit action is visible to the fans in the stands. Running at short tracks like Martinsville as well as on the high-speed superspeedways requires a NASCAR driver to be very versatile.

Certainly one of the most interesting of the dirt tracks in this country is the Pennsboro Motor Speedway near Parkersburg, West Virginia. The track is over 100 years old, and for most of its career it served as a horse track. Several streams wander through the infield area, necessitating several bridges on the track. The fans actually bring shovels to carve out a seat on the side of a mountain to watch the race. The track presents a unique driving challenge to the drivers as well.

Dirt track stock car fans are true race fans. They have to endure a multitude of discomforts to watch the competition on the track. The first rule

is not to wear anything nice, as it will be coated with dust. At many tracks, the wide rear tires of the cars spew gritty dirt into the grandstands, and fans have to endure getting dirt into their eyes, up their noses, and just about everywhere!

These small dirt tracks are the final vestiges of early Americana. To many stock car fans, dirt tracking is the only way real stock car racing should be done. It's a down in the "mud and the blood" situation that the fans love to watch and to be part of.

The popularity of dirt versus pavement racing seems to flip-flop. During the 1970s, the popu-

Below: *The Winchester Motor Speedway in Indiana is the fastest half-mile short track in the country. Its 34-degree banking can produce 120 mile-per-hour lap speeds. Here, ASA drivers Jay Sauter (1) and Lonny Rush Jr. (77) battle on the famed high banks.*

Bottom: *The 100-year-old Pennsboro (West Virginia) Motor Speedway is one of the oldest tracks in the country. A majority of the fans view the race from the side of the mountain overlooking the ancient racing facility. The track now runs only high-dollar special events.*

larity of dirt racing increased to high levels. Some track owners peeled back their black top surfaces and got back to the dirt. Other tracks played it safe and just put dirt down over the pavement.

During the 1980s, the popularity of pavement stock car racing has returned. Several reasons have been cited for that turn-around, the most significant of which is that pavement is much easier to maintain. Dirt tracks require continuous preparation and refurbishment to keep the racing surface competitive and fast.

What the 1990s will bring is hard to guess. Stock car racing is like the wind – unpredictable!

The Crew

Above: *NASCAR crews, or for that matter any crew, must be able to master any contingency while at the track. There are specialists on the crews that can work on all the systems of the car. Here, the crew of NASCAR rookie Derrick Cope replaces the motor in his Purolator Pontiac. Sometimes three or four engines are used in preparing for a race.*

Right: *A crew's work is never done. Extensive race preparation is necessary even after a successful qualifying attempt. Here, Richard Petty's crew gives his STP Pontiac a complete going-over prior to the start of the Goody's 500 at Martinsville Speedway.*

With today's high-tech stock cars, one would think that all the winning is done on the race track: just put that high-performance machine in gear and race for the checkered. Not true! As is the case with a majority of the other types of auto racing, the action that takes place in the pit area many times foretells the winner in stock car racing.

The efficiency of the pit crews, of course, comes into play primarily in the longer races, where numerous stops must be made. On the superspeedways, where each second accounts for almost the distance of a football field by the cars on the track, a half-second here or there can mean the difference between victory and defeat.

The transaction between car and mankind with rubber and fuel replenishment occurs in a crowded and scary place. Richard Petty has indicated on more than one occasion that the pits are the most dangerous place on the track. Much of the danger comes from the fact that with modern racing, when the yellow flag comes out, almost all the cars on the track dive low for the pits. Fancy 15 or 20 cars all trying to be in the same general area at the same time!

Above: *One of the biggest expenses in stock car racing is tires. As many as eight sets of tires may be used by a single team in a superspeedway race. Mounting up to ten sets of tires for up to 42 teams is a mammoth task.*

Right: *Fuel cans can weigh more than 70 pounds each. Since the driver can't pull up to the pump and fill her up, all fuel is dumped in, ten gallons at a time, by a husky fuelman.*

Opposite: *Fast and furious pre-race pit activity preceding the NASCAR race at Bristol (Tennessee) International Raceway. Because of the supreme stresses on the car due to the 36-degree banking, the crews must be ready for suspension and drivetrain problems.*

Then, there's the heat with which to cope. Everything on an almost two-ton stock car is hot after being out on the track. The tires have boiled to over 200°, exhaust pipes radiate with engine heat, and radiators are smoking. Crews must also contend with the ever-present threat of fire. A number of crewmen have been burned in sudden fires through the years, the most recent mishap taking place in the Petty pits at the 1989 Winston Cup race at Atlanta. The King's car was being re-fueled when an apparent engine misfire ignited fuel on the side of the car. Crew member Robert Callicut, who was fortunately wearing a fire suit at

the time, was squarely in the middle of the billow of flame and suffered serious burns to his leg and back.

The brave and highly-skilled men that accomplish these important duties come in many sizes and shapes. They vary from the tailored-uniformed and super-efficient crews of NASCAR to the groups at the smaller tracks in jeans and T-shirts just trying to get the job done. Nevertheless, the job is the same – to keep their stock car on the track operating at maximum efficiency and to perform any maintenance needed to keep it that way.

Opposite: *Darrell Waltrip's crew is one of the best in NASCAR. The colorfully-dressed, Tide-sponsored crew has proven its tremendous capabilities on numerous occasions, and has assisted Waltrip to many victories during the past few years.*

Left: *The Coors Ford Thunderbird is a family operation. Here, two of the Elliott brothers (driver Bill and crew chief Ernie) discuss race set-up during a practice session at Martinsville Speedway. The team finally won the NASCAR Winston Cup Championship in 1988 after coming close for several years.*

Below: *The King (Richard Petty) and a part of his crew contemplate what is to come at another of Petty's hundreds of NASCAR races.*

In NASCAR and ARCA, the pit working area is just 26 feet in length and just slightly wider than the car. Five men are allowed over the wall to service the car when it roars into that tiny area. When cars are on either end of the area, space is tight and there is a virtual explosion of tires, air hoses and fuel cans as the crews work quickly to get their cars back out onto the track. One Winston Cup crewman once joked that it wasn't a good pit stop if at least one lug nut wasn't off a front wheel before the car had stopped. That might be a little exaggerated, but quickness is the keynote of these crews.

Sometimes things don't go right on pit stops, such as when a car overshoots the pit area or comes up short. Either situation is very dangerous to crewmen who might be in the way of an out-of-control car. Crewmen also have to beware of cars that are zooming by as they are working on the right side of their car.

The pressure to get the job done quickly and well is immense. National TV coverage of big NASCAR races often uses a split screen to compare the pit stops of the two leading cars. One mistake by one or the other crew and the whole national television audience is witness to the goof. It's little wonder that the first thanks that usually come from a winning stock car driver are for the work done by his pit crew.

Tire changing is one of the most critical operations performed by the pit crews. Longer races have as many as six tire changes, so doing them quickly becomes that much more important. To that end, the lug nuts are cemented to the outside of the wheel so that when one of the nuts is spun up by an air wrench, it can be snugged up in a hurry. The characteristic whine of those wrenches is very familiar to anyone who has ever watched a race on television.

A NASCAR pit crew in action is a thing of beauty to watch. It's like an automotive ballet, with all of the performers working in perfect unison. Everything happens like clockwork. A precise crew can change two outside tires and pour in two dump cans of fuel in only 12 or 13 seconds. And as the technology of the cars improves every year, so does the technology of the crews doing their jobs. Compared to the way pit stops were performed some 20 years ago, those of today are done in almost half the time.

3 4 5
aston
Series
76
Goody's
Official Pain Reliever of NASCAR
SVILLE
Winston Cup Series
Kodak
RACIN
State
26
GOODY'S 500
Winsto

Previous pages: *Pit stop action ar Martinsville Speedway.*

Right: *Proper weight balance is important in a stock car which is making nothing but right-hand turns. A crewman, with a special ratchet tool, can add or take away weight by either tightening or loosening this mechanism. Stock cars can use up to 60 percent left-side weight.*

Above: *Stock car races can be won or lost in the pits. Everything that the pit crew will have to do must be practiced over and over again. Two dump cans of fuel must be poured into the tank as quickly as possible as the tires are being changed. All this must be done in some 15 seconds in a very intense environment.*

Pit stops in stock car racing could undoubtedly be a lot faster if air jacks like those used with Indy cars were allowed. But the stock car boys still all do it with a good old pump-type jack, and that seems to be the way they want to keep it. The jack is placed in a slot cut out of the lower side of each side of the car.

Not only must the NASCAR pit crews be quick, they must also be tidy. Should a car inadvertently run over an air hose or jack, the car could incur a penalty. Most likely, the car would have to come into the pits and make a quick stop before going back out. This is called a "stop-and-go" penalty. On occasion, cars have left the pits too early with a gas can still hanging in the refueling hole or a jack dangling underneath. There have even been occasions when an over-anxious driver has pulled out before the lug nuts have been tightened

up. Suddenly the driver will find himself trying to get back to the pits on three wheels!

Not only must these unheralded men execute their jobs with finesse, but they must also frequently exercise sheer brute strength. The tireman must vault over the wall with a tire and wheel under each arm. The gas man must go over the wall, manhandling an 80-pound dump can on his shoulder, and swing the can into position to gravity-fill the car with 10 gallons of gas. He's got to go through the same pattern a second time with another can, getting every last drop into the tank as the car comes down off the jack. This is critical, because that last drop could be the difference between the car making it across the finish line and running out of fuel on the last turn.

A pit crew has to be the ultimate in flexibility, in constant readiness for any possible situation. For

Left: *Jacking a car up quickly and precisely is imperative for a good pit stop. A cut-out section on the lower door panel marks the exact spot for the crewman to place the jack. A rivet above the cutout on this particular car centers the jack. These cutouts are located on both sides of the car.*

example, an accident could cause extensive body damage. Most commonly, sheet metal may bend down over a tire causing it to smoke and creating the possibility of a blow-out. Once in the pits, the crews attack such a problem with pry-bars and cutters to clear a path for the tire to roll freely. But for the most part, there's no way to assess in advance what will be needed to repair a car, although the driver, through his two-way communications, can provide some estimate of the problem. Many times, a failure in the engine, transmission or rear end could be a terminal situation, but a crew will try anything to keep its racing machine on the track. Even though a car may lose many laps, at times a crew will have to take a car back to the garage area for extensive repairs. The car will then re-enter the race, even though there's no possibility of winning or even finishing

in the top ten, in order to procure as many points as possible. If the driver is in the final points' race, he could still have a chance of winning the championship.

Many of the NASCAR pit crews have been to-gether for many years. The members are bonded together as a team and work as if they are one man. The most famous of these is the Wood Brothers crew, which seems to have been around forever. In short track racing at the grass roots level, the elaborate pit set-ups of the NASCAR crews just don't exist. Cars often pit in makeshift areas in the infield. Although this lacks the glory and exposure of the big time, the job is the same, and just as important.

There is no schooling for becoming a pit crew-man at the top level. Experience is the best teacher. Crewmen quickly develop a healthy re-

Above: *As the sport of stock car racing has evolved, the efficiency of the pit crews has kept pace. It is not uncommon for two tires to be changed in 14 seconds or less. In NASCAR, the lug nuts are glued onto the wheel to speed the changing process. The whir of the high-speed impact wrenches is a familiar sound as the lug nuts are spun off and on. Although short track races seldom require pit stops, the crews still practice changing tires in case of a flat tire on the track.*

Above: *Haulers for the NASCAR series have become traveling billboards advertising the sponsor's wares. Bill Elliott's hauler sports an air-brushed version of his famous Coors Thunderbird. These amazing haulers attract nearly as much attention as the race cars themselves.*

spect for the inherent danger of their jobs.

Although not technically a part of the pits, the huge haulers that bring everything needed for the race to the track are an integral part of the sport behind-the-scenes. "Hauler" is hardly a fitting name for these amazing semi-machines. The haulers are one of the most exciting aspects of big-time stock car racing, and even for a few of the teams of the smaller circuits. These are beautiful machines, with many sporting tons of chrome and fancy paint schemes.

Many trailers carry complete machine shops, including lathes, drill presses, saws, welders, air compressors, and so on. They also provide a vast area for advertising for the sponsor. Most teams bring two cars to each race, with the spare car stored on top of the other car. The skilled crews can completely change an engine in an unbeliev-ably short time.

Needless to say, a smaller team's equipment is less spectacular. Hauling the car in a closed trailer pulled by a pick-up is first-class to many of these

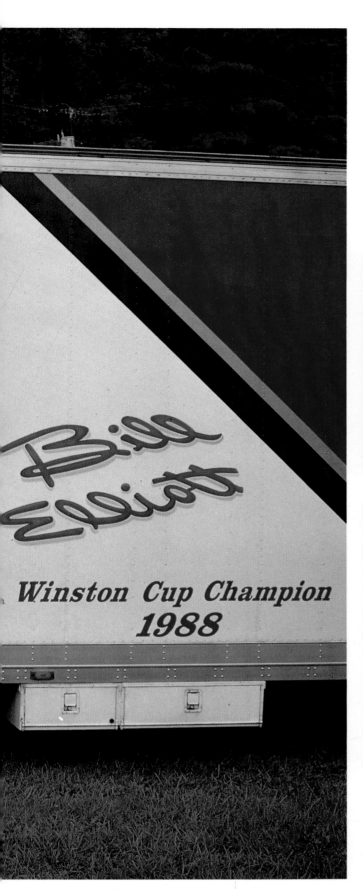

Below: *How's this for exposure of three main stock car sponsors' products? Shown are the Texaco Havoline hauler of Davey Allison, the Tide Machine hauler of Darrell Waltrip, and the Sunoco hauler of Sterling Marlin.*

Middle: *Many haulers have built-in hydraulic ramps. Here, Ricky Rudd's Quaker State Buick is in the process of being unloaded.*

Bottom: *Short track stock car racers normally tow their race cars on open trailers and keep their tools and spare parts in the back of a truck.*

low-budget teams. A favorite and more economical method of transportation is a school bus. Many teams cut off the back half of the bus for the car and then ride to the races up front. Some teams even bring their cars to the race on the back of a wrecker cable. Sometimes that mode of transportation can come in handy after the race!

Some stock car teams definitely live in the fast lane; others just do what is necessary. But they all have the same goal — to get to the track, get the car into competition, and keep it on the track.

The Cars

Stock car. These words mean different things to racing fans from different parts of the country. A stock car can be anything from a magnificent, showy NASCAR Winston Cup machine down to a no-frills $2000 machine built from junkyard parts. Yet underlying every effort is the common theme of a full-bodied, somewhat stock-bodied race car. Recognition from the fans that these are passenger cars being raced against each other is the basis for the continuing popularity of the sport.

However, with the more sophisticated cars, that stock appearance is only skin-deep. Underneath that gleaming exterior, covered with dozens of sponsor's decals, resides a real racing machine. Yet most fans are still interested to know whether a car is a Ford or a Chevy. NASCAR fans also draw solid connections between a driver and a make, such as with Dale Earnhardt and Chevy, and Bill Elliott and Ford.

Back in the early days of the sport, the term "stock" really meant "stock," as in passenger car. This remained true into the 1960s, when stock cars were actually converted from cars that were bought from the showroom floor. Early stock cars used street tires and added a roll cage, with few other variations. In the early 1950s, Detroit began helping the name drivers in NASCAR by providing cars, parts, motors, advice and technology. This trend has continued off and on ever since.

All stock cars are not equal. In fact, about the only common factor is that they all carry fenders. The cars can actually be classified by the organizations with which they race.

Most familiar are the Winston Cup machines that sport the big money, big company brand recognition, big driver names, and big corporate sponsors. One step down are the Busch Grand National machines, which compete in many Winston Cup races. On occasion, Winston Cup drivers use this type of car to compete against the up-and-coming Busch Grand National drivers.

The ARCA cars are very similar to Winston Cup cars, and in fact, many of these cars are former Winston Cup cars carrying different paint schemes. The ASA/ALL-PRO/ARTGO/ACT organizations have their own class of cars. Finally, a broad class of cars comes under the classification of "late models".

Two of the most numerous stock car types are the "mini-stocks" and "street stocks." Both these types of cars go by many different names, but they have a common goal of providing inexpensive stock car racing. At tracks all across the country, these cars are always there ready to run.

Here is a closer look at each of these types.

Winston Cup

One might think that with all the national publicity Winston Cup racing receives that these cars would be the fastest of all the stock car types. This is, however, not true.

These cars weigh in at a beefy 3700 pounds and have severe engine restrictions. Over the years, the maximum engine size allowed in Winston Cup racing has been steadily reduced, with the possibility of further reduction in the future. But even though the power is down, the technology for these cars continues to push on, enabling the teams to keep the speeds up.

Above: *Probably the most famous of all Winston Cup stock cars is the bright blue and red STP-sponsored number 43 machine of Richard Petty. The King has always been number 43, and he has carried the same basic color scheme for many years. Richard is the second in a three-generation racing family.*

Left: *It takes a lot of skilled manpower to keep a Winston Cup car perking to perfection. Michael Waltrip's youthful Country Time Lemonade crew has gained experience and respect during the 1989 Winston Cup campaign.*

Above: *One of the most colorful cars running in NASCAR Winston Cup competition is the flashy Lumina Tide Machine of Darrell Waltrip. This team was one of three in the Hendricks racing stable, along with the teams of Geoff Bodine and Ken Schrader. The team united Waltrip and master crew chief Wadell Wilson. Despite a disappointing initial year, fans knew that it was only a matter of time before this super team fired on all cylinders and became a consistent winner. Success for this team brought a resurgence of popularity and fan support for Waltrip. This team will be one to be reckoned with in the early 1990s.*

Very little "tricking up" is allowed in the contouring of the showroom body lines. The body must conform to the shape of the street model of the same year and brand. The windshield must be at exactly the same angle as the passenger version, along with all the other angles and lines. About the only deviations allowed are larger wheel well openings, to accommodate the large racing wheels, and the small spoiler on the rear deck to keep the car from literally "taking off" when it's running at 200 miles an hour.

More aerodynamic grooming appears on these cars every year, thanks to the factories themselves, and the NASCAR drivers take full advantage of these super-slick machines and the thrilling ride they give. The teams take great care in preparing the cars to make sure that there are no open seams in the sheet metal, where a tiny bit of air could get trapped and slow the car a hundredth of a mile per hour. Every little thing counts when every car is equal. High technology has definitely come to stock car racing in many ways. Even aircraft wind tunnels have now come into play in NASCAR, as the teams look for that extra little edge. The tunnels are able to simulate speeds to the maximum capability of the car in order to determine if flaws exist in the design.

The NASCAR organization makes sure that no teams work outside the rules. The organization uses factory body templates before every race. Every car is carefully measured before each race to ensure conformity. More than one team in the past has been sent back to "straighten things out a bit" before the car is allowed to race.

Racing has played an important role in the design of cars during the 1980s. A look at the designs of Ford and General Motors shows that they are looking more and more like race cars with every passing year.

A race car speeding forward is extremely sensitive to wind. The force slowing a car down is called drag. The unit used to measure the efficiency of a stock car's body shape is called its coefficient of drag, or C_D. The lower the C_D, the more efficient the design. NASCAR Winston Cup cars have very low C_Ds — less than .30.

The engines which push these sleek machines are either 350-cubic-inch General Motors' or 351-cubic-inch Fords. These are specially-prepared racing engines and cost about $25,000 each. Most are rebuilt between each race.

Engines are even prepared differently for different tracks. The most significant differential is whether the engine will be used on a long or short

Below: *Even though the Busch Grand National cars use V-6 powerplants, the competition is still speedy and tough. The cars serve as an excellent proving ground for aspiring Winston Cup drivers. This action photo shows Kenny Wallace (36) dueling with Jack Ingram (11).*

track. Also, the remainder of the powertrains are specifically built for racing. Finally, the rear end gearing will also vary depending on track length.

The cumulative effects of improved suspensions, engines and aerodynamics have continued to push the performance of these cars ever higher. In 1988, NASCAR made an attempt to slow the cars down on the superspeedways by downgrading the engine power with a special carburetor restricter plate which trimmed off some 200 horsepower. The experiment nearly ended after 1989, as the drivers complained that they needed the extra power to accelerate in order to escape accidents.

The brand identification of a Winston Cup race car is important, but underneath that shiny metal beats the heart of a pure race car. Holding everything in place is a welded tubular steel frame that protects the driver on all sides. Heavy horizontal tubing protects the door area in case of a "T-bone" hit like that received by Bobby Allison in his serious 1988 accident. A complete integral roll cage surrounds the driver. NASCAR Winston Cup machines in the past have rolled over many times with the driver walking away. Passenger cars would certainly benefit from such an added safety measure in the design.

Busch Grand National

Busch Grand National cars look a lot like their Winston Cup big brothers, but significant differences exist beneath the hood. Busch Grand National cars are lighter than the Winston Cup cars, weighing only 3200 pounds. Most of the cars use V-6 engines as opposed to the more powerful V-8 engines found in Winston Cup cars, although Winston Cup machines may soon also be using the V-6 powerplants. This trend toward the use of V-6 engines is now dominating the automotive industry, and will probably soon be visible in stock car racing.

Like their Winston Cup brothers, the Grand National cars also use a number of different body styles, such as Buick, Oldsmobile, Pontiac and Ford. The Grand National series provides outstanding racing which looks just like the big time, but serves as a learning situation for up-and-coming drivers. NASCAR has also recently experimented with another stock car division which uses Winston Cup cars in which the engines have been downgraded by using a two-barrel carburetor instead of the normal four-barrel unit. This decrease in the power of the engine gives a young driver a better chance to learn the peculiarities of the car.

Top: *One of the up-and-coming stars of the Busch Grand National series is young Kenny Wallace, brother of 1989 NASCAR Winston Cup Champion Rusty Wallace. Kenny started his racing career as a pit crewman before becoming a driver with the American Speed Association in the 1980s. He will undoubtedly become a Winston Cup driver in the 1990s.*

Above: *Busch Grand National cars run on many short tracks in the Midwest and South. Prior to the start of the feature race, the cars are lined up on the main straightaway, the drivers are introduced individually, and the fans cheer for their favorite drivers. Driver recognition is important in all types of stock car racing.*

Right: *Chuck Bown (63) and Winston Cupper Rick Mast (22) race into the third turn at the Louisville Motor Speedway, one of the premier short tracks in America. Busch Grand National racing is close and exciting, and these drivers aren't afraid to swap paint. The action closely resembles that of Winston Cup racing.*

Bottom: *ARCA race cars are very similar to those of the Winston Cup. The series allows the cars to be up to five years old. Bob Brevak's Race Glaze Buick, shown here, would be a welcome addition to any racing series.*

Below: *Sponsorship is extremely important in modern stock car racing. Companies pay contingency money when their decals are displayed and their products are used. This ARCA car shows a typical decal alignment.*

ARCA

Like the NASCAR stock cars, the racing machines of the ARCA series also maintain their stock appearance with the normal exception of the wheel-well cut-outs and rear deck spoiler. The series is interesting in that it allows, and even encourages, older cars to compete. Through the years, many former Winston Cup stock cars have been sold by their original owners and raced in ARCA for a number of years. Cars up to five years old are allowed to compete.

Both V-6 and V-8 powerplants are allowed in ARCA competition in these 3400-pound cars. Many of the ARCA teams have both short track and superspeedway cars, which are expensive to maintain, but necessary in order to compete. Many different brands of cars compete in ARCA; in 1989 a Chrysler was introduced, the first to race in many years. This could point to the return of the Chrysler brand to big-time stock car racing.

ASA/All-Pro/ARTGO/ACT

The rules for the cars of these sanctioning bodies make them a different breed from the NASCAR and ARCA machines, but they are certainly no less sophisticated.

These cars have body lines which match their street counterparts exactly, except that their bodies are constructed of fiberglass rather than sheet metal.

Both V-8 and V-6 powerplants are allowed, but cubic-inch restrictions on both types keep the competition close. Other restrictions include the use of a very low 9-1 compression ratio for the engines and a small carburetor. These restrictions keep the engines out of the super-high-performance category and allow them to "live" for hundreds of laps without failure.

Left: *These cars use small block, low-compression (9-1) powerplants. The engine is set back several inches for better weight balance. A small carburetor allows these engines to live for hundreds of laps.*

Below: *The magnificent '89 Thunderbird of Lonny Rush Jr. looks like a showcar. These cars don't stay this clean for long, as this close-in, bump-and-run racing is really hard on the fiberglass bodies.*

Late Models

This generic stock car term covers a wide range of racing machines across the country. Almost every track has late models, and it would be impossible to find two tracks with exactly the same late models.

A vast majority of these cars are run by small-team operations which are supported by volunteer crews and spend many long nights working on their cars. Usually, everybody has another job, and the work is done in somebody's garage after hours. This is a tough way to do it, but most of the teams love stock car racing enough to find a way to get their cars ready for the next race.

Most of the cars are of sheet metal construction, sometimes with a plastic nosepiece. A late model can end up costing as much as $30,000, with about half of the cost in the motor and half in the car.

Depending on the particular track or sanctioning body, the auto bodies can vary from having to be very close to stock lines to just about "anything goes." In some situations, large deck-mounted wings are allowed, along with square

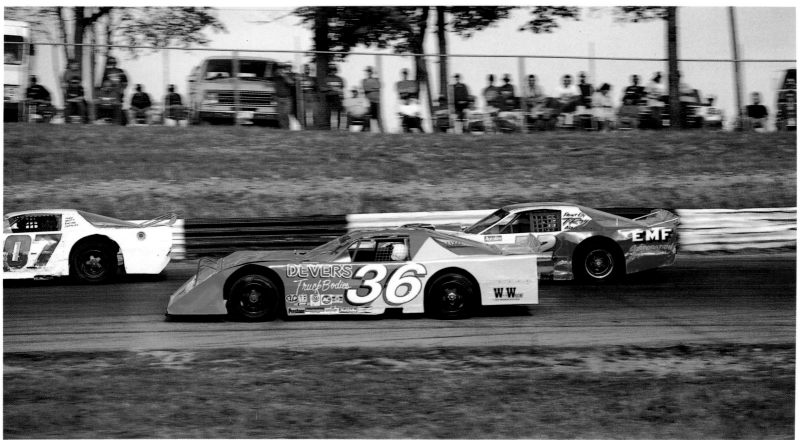

Bottom: *Two different styles of late models race at the Winchester (Indiana) Speedway. The number 44 car is the more traditional-style late model, whereas the number 67 car is the more aerodynamic wedge-style design. Fan popularity is split about 50-50 between the two types of body styles.*

Below: *The 114 car demonstrates a combination of the traditional and wedge body styles with the use of a front air dam and a rear fender extension and plastic wing. The car also shows the good looks that many late models strive for in modern racing.*

slab sides and long aerodynamic noses. This variation in rules can cause problems when a driver wants to compete at more than one track. Many times it's necessary to snip off a portion of a wing or shorten a skirt in order to make a car legal.

Most late models use V-8 engines of varying sizes, although many of the drivers feel that the V-6 powerplant will become more popular in this realm of stock car racing in the 1990s. Most of the cars also have full tubular racing chassis' and sophisticated suspension systems with special racing coil-over shocks.

Keeping a late model running demands a great deal of time and effort. This is grass roots racing, where the driver himself is a part of the crew down there in the mud and dust working on the car.

Some late models compete on pavement and some on dirt. As a rule, the dirt late models tend to have more radical body styles and also have a tendency to show more wear and tear due to the harsh nature of dirt racing. Recently, some drivers have experimented with running dirt late models on pavement, making for some pretty exciting racing.

Above: *Ford Pintos are one of the most popular cars used as mini-stockers. They are aerodynamic, readily available, inexpensive and easy to work on. This particular car is the very successful mount of Cincinnati female driver Kim Young.*

Top right: *Mini-stock action on the high banks of Winchester (Indiana) Speedway is pedal-to-the-metal all the way around. Donnie Jeschke in the number 99 car hangs the rear end out while passing the number 7 car of Rick Manion.*

Center right: *Three tightly-bunched Pinto mini-stockers scream through turn two at Kil-Kare Speedway in Xenia, Ohio. Mini-stockers are very popular in the Midwest.*

Bottom right: *Street stock racing is a popular and inexpensive way to get started in stock car racing. These are basically street cars with safety modifications. A driver can get into this style of racing for minimal money expenditure.*

Mini-Stocks

Short track stock car racing in America is getting to be a very expensive sport, and is actually getting beyond the means of many drivers and owners. Many teams simply cannot afford to keep up a late model car anymore. A viable alternative is the mini-stock. Although these little cars have low power, low weight and low cost, they are quite high on excitement.

Such now-extinct passenger models as Vega and Pinto are popular body styles for these cars. Since the motor in these cars must match the body style, the Pinto body and motor seems to be the favored combination.

Most mini-stock teams make very little change to the bodies because the factory aerodynamics work well at the speeds at which these cars run. Since thousands of these cars were produced, they are readily available in junkyards and don't present a high-cost problem. Most builders of mini-stocks remove the rear window for airflow through the car. These machines may not be running at 200 miles per hour, but every little bit still helps on the short tracks where these cars run.

Most mini-stock teams bore their engines out slightly and install larger valves. The addition of headers and a bigger carb in a powerplant can sometimes double the horsepower. The remainder of a typical mini-stock powertrain consists of the stock four-speed transmission and rear end. Detroit certainly never had such activities in mind for these cars when they were built, but these little movers continue to grow in numbers as the financial attractiveness of these machines catches on.

These mini-stock cars don't do their racing in front of thousands of fans or appear on national TV. They race locally, before a local crowd, and this is what stock car racing has become in many parts of the country. In the 1990s, it could well become the standard for the stock car sport.

Bottom: *Just about every age and body style of car can be seen in street stock racing. One of the interesting aspects of racing in this class is that there is no indication of the speed capability of each race car. Many times, the most battered-looking race car will take the checkered flag.*

Below: *Street stocks run on both pavement and dirt racing surfaces. Although dirt is slicker, it is also more forgiving. Here, two street stockers do a little fender-bending during action at Eldora Speedway in Rossburg, Ohio. Both cars continued without significant damage.*

Street Stocks

One has to start somewhere in stock car racing and, for this purpose, street stocks are ideal. A complete car that was hauled from the junkyard provides the basics, to which are added just the bare essentials necessary to get the machine around the track. In many cases, a sum as low as $2000 could put such a car on the race track.

Many of these street stocks — also known as hobby stockers, Detroit Iron, bombers, and the like — are 1970s-style full-bodied cars. The interior is gutted and a roll bar, which is usually required, is added. These are the only real signs that this is a racing stock car. Fancy paint schemes are expensive, so spraybomb coatings with shaky hand-lettering, which are much more cost-effective, are often all that decorates these primitive racing machines.

On many tracks, in order to keep the cost down, the cars are run on street tires. This is "square one" racing, where a driver can decide whether he likes the sport well enough to move on in the future.

Behind the Wheel

Driving a stock car is exciting beyond belief. Imagine having a vehicle that's built for speed, and a situation where it's legal to drive it as fast as it will go!

Everything about a stock car speaks of speed and high performance. But the setting for all this excitement is not luxurious. The inside of a stock car is pretty bleak – no velour or chrome here. The car is comfortable, though, in a different way. Imagine you're in the driver's seat. You fit in snugly, with heavy racing belts holding you in place. You sit low in the car – almost too low, it seems. You can't even see over the hood and you wonder how real race drivers put these machines to peak performance.

When the engine is fired, the noise pulsates through the car and your body. The throaty, deep sound builds up the level of excitement. Suddenly it hits you that you're going to get to put all those throbbing ponies to work for you. You can hardly wait to give it a shot.

On the track, it's a blast! It seems so fast. You just know that you could take that checkered flag the first time out. "Hey, this is easy. Just punch that pedal to the floor and let her rip," you think.

But that's certainly not the case for any type of modern stock car. These are intricate, high-tech machines requiring a skilled and experienced chauffeur behind the wheel. And even then, many times even the famous-name drivers will spin out or even put the car into the wall.

No matter what type of stock car, track surface or track length is involved, several special terms apply to the handling and maneuvering of all modern stock cars. The two main challenges a driver must face on the track are in controlling the car when it is **pushing**, and when it is **loose**. A car which is pushing wants to keep going straight instead of turning, which is natural when a car is going forward at a high speed. When a car is loose, its rear end seems to want to pass its front end. Some drivers intentionally set up their cars on the loose side to fit their particular driving style.

Crews use several techniques to make the cars easier to handle. One of these, known as playing with the **stagger**, means that the diameter of the tires on the outside of the car is different from those on the inside of the car. If all the tires were the same diameter, the car would be very **tight**, or hard to handle on a banked track. The car can be loosened up by inflating the right-side tires to a

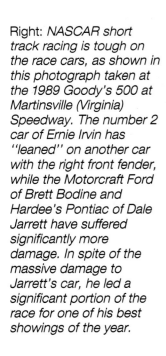

Right: *NASCAR short track racing is tough on the race cars, as shown in this photograph taken at the 1989 Goody's 500 at Martinsville (Virginia) Speedway. The number 2 car of Ernie Irvin has "leaned" on another car with the right front fender, while the Motorcraft Ford of Brett Bodine and Hardee's Pontiac of Dale Jarrett have suffered significantly more damage. In spite of the massive damage to Jarrett's car, he led a significant portion of the race for one of his best showings of the year.*

Below: *A majority of the short track late models use Chevy powerplants and sheet metal, because of the availability of replacement parts and the more reasonable cost of the equipment. Many times, though, it's difficult to tell exactly what brand a particular car is trying to represent. Once in a while a Ford does get into the late model fray, as seen by the number 23 car in this action.*

larger circumference, which makes up for the banking of the track. The difference in circumference between the tires can be as much as an inch or more. Crew members can constantly be seen measuring the tire stagger with a metal tape which is inserted into a hole in the tire.

The term **bite** refers to an adjustment which can be made to a stock car by increasing the stiffness of the car's front end springs. Tightening up the springs gives the car more bite. Loosening up the springs brings **wedge** to the car, which helps to control push and looseness.

In stock car lingo, "hooked up" means that everything is exactly right on the car. A "dailed in" car means about the same thing. Everything is exactly perfect — don't touch a thing. A "trick set-up" means that something in a particular machine is making it go faster. Of course, when a car really starts moving unexpectedly there is always the suspicion that something is being done that's illegal.

Many other factors help the driver control a stock car. Since a stock car is always running counterclockwise on the track, it's logical that the left side of the car should be heavier to make it handle better. On dirt, the car is less sensitive to added left-side weight, while pavement cars run well with up to 60 percent of the weight on the left side of the car.

Other considerations include roll centers, spring rates, front-to-rear weight distribution, and on and on. High technology has definitely come to stock car racing. Now all that's needed for this perfectly-tuned high-performance machine is a driver. Ready to give it a try?

First, start thinking whether you are driving on a long or a short track. On the small paved ovals, the cars are actually in a continuous slide all the way around. That's a pretty exciting situation when you consider that many times two or three cars are running side by side in that condition. Many veteran drivers say, though, that this is not difficult to do if you have confidence in the guy running alongside you.

One fact about driving a car on a short track is that it's very crowded out there. One slip by a driver can make things real interesting in a big hurry. At these close quarters, a lot of cars are likely to be quickly involved, with a lot of sheet metal bent as a result. Many times, the slower

speed of the smaller tracks will prevent major damage to the cars, but not always. It's easy to understand this statement once made about full-size stock cars running on small ''bull ring'' tracks: ''It's like flying fighter planes in a high school gym!''

Short tracker extraordinaire John Vallo says that not all is lost if you get hit in one of these short track encounters: ''If your car is set up right, you can sometimes keep the car from spinning out or hitting the wall. If the car is not right, most likely you won't be able to keep it under control. The worst place to get hit in these cars is in the rear end.

''Then there's the situation of trying to recover from that spin after you've been tagged. Your reaction time in responding is everything in this situation. Sometimes you can pull out the car by staying on the gas,'' Vallo explained. Sometimes it's not so easy.

Things happen quickly when you're in a stock car on a short track. No sooner have you exited one turn then you have to start setting up the car for the next turn. Some short tracks really don't have any straightaways, so the car seems to be turning all the time. This makes passing very hard indeed.

Gauging the exact location of the car is very difficult, since you are sitting so low in the car. No wheel-to-wheel racing here, like in Indy cars. Heck, it's not possible when you can't even see the wheels! Racing on a track is a lot harder than driving the Los Angeles Freeway at 100 miles per hour. On the race track, every car has the same goal – to get to the front. As one driver noted, ''It's very important to think about all the cars that are behind you.'' No turn signals or brake lights exist to warn other cars of your intentions. That's why it's imperative not to make any radical, unexpected maneuvers.

Above: *Kyle Petty (42) and Larry Pearson (16) are trading a little sheet metal in this innocent-looking incident. Both cars are out of the groove and seemingly out of harm's way. The smoke from the rear of Petty's car is from the locked rear tires sliding on the pavement.*

Sooner or later, though, that hard crash into the wall is unavoidable. What usually happens is that the race car ends up about two feet shorter than before. Most drivers will tell you that they try not to think about having an accident on the track. "You can't think about it out there when you are running at speed," says Vallo. "That takes your mind off the driving business at hand. These cars are built well these days and can take a head-on shot and you can walk away from it most of the time. The worst thing about having a heavy hit is waiting for it to happen. It seems to take forever for that crunch to happen.

"But the worst thing that can happen to you in a stock car is to be 'T-boned,' says Vallo. 'That's when you get hit in the driver's door by another car. It's a good way to get killed and was the circumstance of Bobby Allison's 1988 crash at the Pocono Speedway.''

Many drivers say that they really forget about the speed of the cars in the heat of short track competition. Everybody out there is running at about the same speed, so the speed is measured by how much faster or slower another car is running than yourself. "It's like running on a merry-go-round," one short track driver explained.

With the flurry of cars all around you, the noise and excitement, it's easy to let your emotions get away from you. "If you get upset out there, you're going to screw up. You just can't do as well and there is the possibility that you will try to drive over your head," a short track stock car driver once explained.

Short track stock car racing presents some tough challenges to the driver. The first is an effect called centrifugal force. That's the pull outward on the driver's body as the car makes high-speed turns. Imagine the force on the neck and head

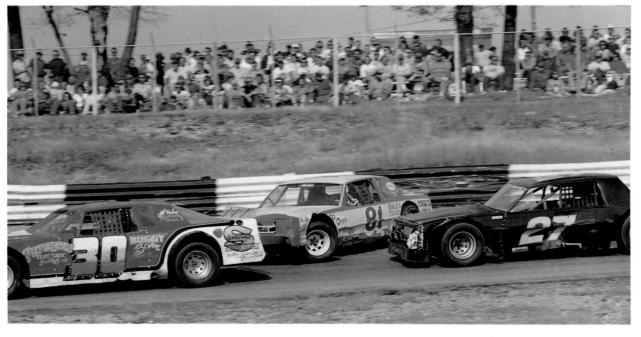

Above: *As Kyle Petty and Larry Pearson straighten their cars out and race on, Davey Allison in the number 28 Havoline Ford locks up his brakes and spins in front of an oncoming Rusty Wallace in number 27, Derrick Cope in number 10 and Ken Schrader in number 25. Allison spun onto the infield grass and lost several laps while trying to get back into the race in this 1989 Martinsville action.*

Left: *In spite of the appearance of impending disaster in this photo, no contact was made.*

Left: *There's nothing like a high-speed traffic jam on a short track to make things interesting. This type of action brings capacity crowds out to just about every NASCAR Winston Cup event.*

Below: *The fast way around the high banks of the Winchester (Indiana) Speedway is up near the wall. However, this late model driver came a bit too close, as he scrapes along the outside wall.*

after driving three or four hundred laps! Many drivers actually use straps attached to their helmets to help combat the force. These G forces have caused many drivers to take up conditioning programs to help overcome the effect.

The 36-degree high banks of the half-mile Bristol (Tennessee) Speedway provide the greatest G forces of any NASCAR track. The shocks squeeze an amazing four inches on the cars and the drivers feel well over two Gs. It's certainly not surprising to see drivers totally exhausted after running those cliffs for 500 laps. It's the ultimate physical challenge, and proves that stock car drivers are real athletes.

The driver's seat is a hot seat in more ways than one. A multi-layer Nomex driving uniform can be pretty uncomfortable when the track temperature is radiating at 120 degrees or higher. The exhaust pipe runs right under the floor, keeping things even toastier. Little wonder that drivers have been known to collapse after getting out of their cars. At times on hot summer days at long NASCAR races, some drivers ask for a relief driver. Being in good physical condition is the key to overcoming the effects of heat and fatigue.

Overleaf: *Mark Martin in the Stroh's Light Thunderbird has the inside track on the Quaker State Buick of Ricky Rudd. The inside groove is usually the fast way around on a slightly-banked short track. Martin is always tough on the short tracks, thanks to his many years of experience with the American Speed Association. The 1989 season was Martin's best ever, as he came very close to winning a Winston Cup Championship. Both of these drivers have large fan followings and are well-respected by fellow competitors.*

Left: *Seems like a shame to mess up a pretty paint job, but that's the price a car has to pay for mortal combat on a short track. In the lower ranks of stock car racing, a car might remain in this condition all season, whereas in NASCAR, this car would be reskinned between races. Sponsors like their cars to look clean.*

Above: *The ravages of war. Modern stock cars have many fiberglass pieces, which easily splinter away when contact occurs on the track. The front clip from this Busch Grand National car was discarded after an accident at the Bristol International Raceway.*

Right: *C. J. Rayburn is one of the kings of dirt late model racing. Not only does he race, but he is also a master car builder in his own right, and builds many cars for the top dirt runners.*

Below: *Randy Boggs, number 17, was the winner of the 1987 World 100. His brother Jack is also a noted late model driver. In this Eldora Speedway action, Randy leads the number 1 car of C. J. Rayburn.*

Dirt stock drivers face a lot of the same problems, but differences do exist. The speeds aren't quite as high, but other factors make it just as challenging, if not more so, than pavement racing.

Just take a look at the way many dirt late model stock cars go through the turns. The rear ends appear to have swung around, giving the impression that the cars are out of control. But that strange orientation is quite by design. By traversing in this strange attitude, the cars can keep up their momentum and the drivers can keep the pedal down all the way around. Needless to say, it's a fine line to keep the cars from spinning out.

Driver visibility is low in a dirt stock car. Most races take place at night, and flying dirt can make seeing almost impossible. Fancy driving at 100 miles per hour in a dust storm with two dozen other cars out there somewhere. No wonder they call these guys the Last American Heroes!

Top: *This number 44 late model demonstrates a loose condition, which is not unusual when driving on dirt.*

Above: *Number 27, Russ Petro, power-slides through the turn at Eldora Speedway. This super-fast track, which sports extremely tall high banks, tests the racing reflexes of even the most skilled dirt driver.*

Below: *The World 100 at Eldora Speedway is the grand-daddy of all late model dirt stock car races. In 1989, the winner took home $25,000. The race annually draws some 200 cars and about 15,000 fans to the tiny western Ohio town of Rossburg.*

Below: *The fastest way to get a dirt late model stock car around a dirt track is to swing the rear end around as if it is trying to pass the front end, as driver John Lawhorn is demonstrating here.*

Bottom: *Hot laps prior to the race often provide some of the best racing of the night. The testing also allows the crew chiefs to set the cars up accurately for that night's racing.*

Previous pages: *Dirt late model superstar Scott Bloomquist demonstrates the fine art of passing on the inside in this 1989 action. The 1988 winner of the World 100 dirt race, he is one of the real comers in the dirt sport.*

Below right: *Certain NASCAR drivers are tremendously popular with the fans. Here, fan favorite Richard Petty autographs a fan's T-shirt.*

Far right: *The thrill of high-speed superspeedway action at Daytona brings out huge crowds year after year.*

Overleaf: *The pits have been called the most dangerous location in racing. Here, pit crews signal the location of their pits. The cars will roar down pit row at over 70 miles per hour.*

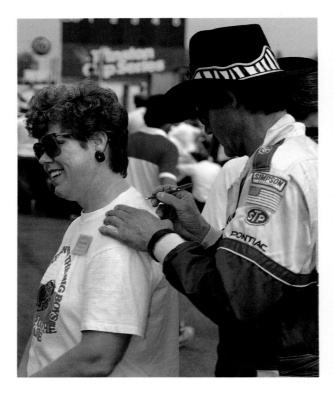

Superspeedway driving is a completely different world. NASCAR and ARCA teams that run the big tracks have what they call "speedway cars" for the Daytona, Charlotte, and Michigan-type speedways.

The big difference is, of course, the speed—double that or more than that of the short tracks. ARCA two-time national champion Marvin Smith said, "It takes a number of laps to get used to it (the speed) that first time. I still remember my first time on a superspeedway. You really have to change your way of thinking at these speeds. Sure, you feel it, and know that you're going real fast. And you had better not forget it for a second.

"At the real high-speed tracks like Talladega, the car tends to move around a lot. It seems to have a mind of its own out there. Then there's the deal of coming into the pits. If you lose a sense of your speed, you'll come in too fast every time."

Another driver explained, "It's a scary situation coming into the pits. You think that you have slowed down, but there's still a blur of pit signs from all of the crews. It's wild as you look for your pit and try to get into that tiny area without hitting anybody. It's equally as dangerous pulling out, because there might be another car nearby with the same idea, or there is also the possibility of a car coming into his pits."

Winston Cup Se
HANES
Kodak
RACIN
MARTINS
17
Budweiser
GM
Goodwrench
Tide
Winston Cup Official
Winston Classic

Left: *The excitement and intensity of the start of a race always brings the fans to their feet. Fast qualifier Dale Earnhardt leads the field into turn one at the 1989 Goody's 500 at Martinsville Speedway.*

Opposite bottom: *Extreme care is necessary when exiting the pits and getting back into racing action. Terry Labonte, number 11, must stay low on the track until he is up to racing speed.*

Below: *The pace car leads a throng of Winston Cup stars before the start of a race at the Talladega Motor Speedway.*

Drafting is an important technique in super-speedway driving. This is the art of using the car ahead of you to help your car along for free. All stock car fans have seen a freight train of ten to twelve NASCAR stockers running nose-to-tail, and there is in fact a scientific reason for this apparent madness. A stock car at speed creates a low pressure, low drag area in which a trailing car can actually "get out of the wind." Letting off the throttle a little in a drafting situation helps to conserve fuel while maintaining speed. While in the drafting position, the trailing car can sometimes — when circumstances permit — pull out of line and "sling-shot" past the car ahead. This maneuver has been accomplished a number of times on the last lap of NASCAR Winston Cup races. In fact, many NASCAR drivers will tell you that they'd rather be in second place tucked in behind the leader starting that last lap. Many times they are able to make the pass for the win.

Overleaf: *Two of the best and most consistent Fords in Winston Cup competition are the machines of Mark Martin (number 6) and Alan Kulwicki (number 7). Martin won his first Winston Cup race in 1989, after several second and third place finishes. He finished third in the final points. Kulwicki seems to be best at qualifying but is seldom around at the end of the race. He turned down a very lucrative offer in order to continue to run his own team.*

Here are just a few of the many stars of stock car racing in America:

Top left: *Rusty Wallace, winner of the 1989 Winston Cup title. He came close in 1988 when he finished second to Bill Elliott.*

Top right: *The Bandit – that's what Harry Gant's many fans call him. Actor Burt Reynolds was part owner of Harry's NASCAR stock car for many years.*

Center left: *The Busch Grand National Champion in 1988, Tommy Ellis has been driving stock cars for 20 years and has over 150 feature wins. He has driven in Winston Cup, but in the late 1980s he concentrated on the Busch series.*

Center right: *Larry Moore's long career has spanned both open wheel and stock car racing. One of the best dirt late model drivers in the country, he has won the World 100 three times.*

Bottom left: *Teenager Donnie Jeschke started his career driving quarter midgets before graduating to mini-stocks. In only his second year in the cars, he won the 1989 track championship at Shady Bowl Speedway in Ohio.*

Bottom right: *Extremely effective in her mini-stock, Kim Young is one of a growing number of females getting into stock car racing.*

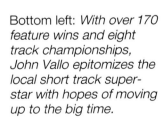

Top left: *Winner of the 1986 Daytona 500, Geoff Bodine has career earnings of some four million dollars. He is known for his track savvy, and has six Winston Cup wins.*

Top right: *One of the young lions of the sport, Rob Moroso has a bright future in Winston Cup racing. He was the 1989 Busch Grand National Champion.*

Center left: *Donnie Moran is one of the kings of dirt late model racing. He dominated the big-money dirt races in 1989 and won the World 100 extravaganza that year.*

Center right: *The only other three-time winner of the World 100 beside Larry Moore is Jeff Purvis. Following a growing trend, Jeff is stepping up to the Busch Grand National series in 1990.*

Bottom left: *With over 170 feature wins and eight track championships, John Vallo epitomizes the local short track super-star with hopes of moving up to the big time.*

Bottom right: *The current king of ASA short track drivers, Butch Miller is known for his expert car set-ups. Butch acquired a 1990 Winston Cup full-time ride and sponsorship.*

Above: *In the 1940s and 1950s, stock cars used to race on the sand of Daytona Beach. Then, in 1959, the Daytona International Speedway was built. This magnificent monument to stock car racing is still considered the Indy 500 of the sport.*

Everything happens very fast at 200 miles per hour. Although the extra distance would seem to allow for more time to deal with any potential problems than on the short tracks, the higher speeds take away that advantage. The drivers are looking about 200 yards ahead, but distance can be sucked up in less than two seconds with a stock car at speed. The first sign of trouble ahead is usually the tire smoke from an out-of-control car. The driver must then make an instantaneous decision on a plan of action — and hope it's right.

During the 1980s, the computer age came to stock car racing. Computers can figure out how much fuel the car is using and tell the driver to throttle back when fuel is running low. Computers also provide data for setting up the car on a particular track. A lot of old-time stock car drivers say this has taken all the fun out of racing, but the computer is going to continue to play an ever-increasing role in stock car racing in the 1990s, just as it is in other aspects of our lives.

Driving a stock car is exciting beyond your wildest dreams. It's a thrill, though, that few of us will ever be able to experience. About the best we can expect is to settle down in front of the TV on a Sunday afternoon and watch those brave warriors go to war on the track. Stock car racing is America's sport!

Above: *The newest speedway in the country, the Louisville Motor Speedway, hosts the NASCAR Busch Grand National cars. This pace car shot shows the forming up of the cars for a 1989 race.*

Left: *The thrill of victory. All the toiling and testing finally came to fruition for Darrell Waltrip in the Goody's 500 race at Martinsville in 1989.*

Index

(Numerals in italics indicate illustrations)

Allison, Bobby, 37, 54
Allison, Davey, 12, *33, 55*
All-Pro, 12, 34
All-Stars, 13
American-Canadian Tour (ACT), 12, 34
American Speed Association (ASA), 12, *17, 26, 34, 37, 40, 58-9*
Andretti, Mario, 13
ARTGO, 12, 34, 40
Atlanta, GA track, 17, 22
Automobile Racing Club of America (ARCA), 12, 26; cars, 34, *39,* 39, 40, 68

Barkdell, Phil, *3-6*
Bloomquist, Scott, *66-7*
Bodine, Brett, *46-7*
Bodine, Geoff, *3-6, 36, 50-1, 52, 77*
body styles, 36, 40, 42-3, *43,* 44, 45. See also specific designs and makes.
Boggs, Jack, *62-3*
Boggs, Randy, *62-3*
Bowen, Chuck, *38*
Brevak, Bob, *39*
Bristol (TN) International Raceway, *23,* 57, *61*
Buick, *33,* 37, *39, 58-9*
Busch Grand National, 12, 34, *37,* 38, *76, 77*; cars, 34, 37, *37, 38, 61, 79*

Cain, Bob, 134
Callicut, Robert, 22
CDs, 36
Charlotte, NC speedway, 68
Chevrolet, 34, *48;* Camaro, 12, *40*
Chrysler, *12-13,* 39; Plymouth, 16
Columbus (OH) Motor Speedway, *17*
computers, 78
Cope, Derrick, *20-1, 55*
Country Time Lemonade crew, *35*

Darlington, SC Speedway, 15
Daytona 500, *13, 77*
Daytona International Speedway, *3-6,* 12, *15,* 15, 17, 68, *68-9, 78*
dirt track racing, 13, 14, 17, 18, 19, 43, *45,* 45, *62, 64, 65, 66-7, 77*
Dodge Daytona, *12-13*
drafting, *14,* 73

Earnhardt, Dale, 11, 34, *72-3*
Eldora Speedway (Rossburg, OH), 13, *45, 62-3, 63, 64-5*
Elliott, Bill, *1,* 10, *25, 32,* 34, *76*
Elliott, Ernie, *25*
Ellis, Tommy, *76*
engines, *20-1,* 34, 36, 37, 40, *41,* 44; V-6, 37, 39, 40, 43; V-8, 39, 40, 43

Firecracker 400, Daytona 1989, *3-6*

Ford, 10, *11, 12,* 34, 36, 37, *48, 74-5;* Havoline, *55;* Mercury, 12; Model T, 14; Motorcraft, *46-7;* Pinto, *44,* 44; Thunderbird, *25, 32-3, 41, 58-9*
Foyt, A J, 13
France, Bill Sr, 10, 11, 15
fueling, *22,* 27, 30, *30*

Gant, Harry, *27, 76*
General Motors, 36
Goody's 500, *20, 46-7, 72-3, 78-9*
Grand National series, 11. *See also* Winston Cup.

haulers, 32, *32, 33;* Quaker State, *33;* Sunoco, *33;* Texas Havoline, *33;* Tide Machine, *33*

Indianapolis Raceway Park, *16,* 26
Indy competitions, *12,* 13, 30, 53, *78*
Ingram, Jack, *37*
Irvin, Ernie, *47*

jacks, 30, *31*
Jarrett, Dale, *46-7*
Jeschke, Donnie, *44, 76*
Johnson, Junior, *12*
Jones, Parnelli, *12*

Kil-Kare Speedway, Xenia, OH, *44*
Kulwicki, Alan, *1, 50-1, 52, 74-5*

Labonte, Terry, *72*
late models, 34, 42, *42, 43, 43, 48, 57, 62, 63, 64, 65, 66-7, 77*
Lawhorn, John, 65
Lorenzen, Freddy, *11,* 12
Louisville Motor Speedway, 17, *38, 49, 79*
Lumina Tide Machine, *36*

Manion, Rick, *44*
Marcum, John, 12
Marlin, Sterling, *3-6, 33*
Martin, Mark, *58-9, 74-5*
Martinsville (VA) Speedway, *1, 18-19, 20,* 25, *29-30, 46-7, 50-1, 52, 55, 72-3, 78-9*
Mast, Russell, *38*
Midwest Association of Race Cars (MARC), 12
Miller, Butch, *40, 77*
mini-stocks, 34, 44, *44,* 76
Moody, Ralph, 10
Moore, Larry, *76, 77*
Moran, Donnie, *77*
Moroso, Rob, *77*

National Association for Stock Car Racing (NASCAR), 10, 11, *11,* 12, 14, 15, 17, 18, *18-9, 20-1,* 22, *23, 24, 25,* 26, 27, 30, *31,* 31, *32,* 34, 37, 39, 40, *46-7,* 57, *60-1, 68,* 68. *See also* Winston Cup, Busch Grand National.
New Bremen, OH Speedway, 14

Oldsmobile, 37, *52*

Parsons, Benny, 12
Parkersburg, W VA, 18
Parsons, Phil, *52*
pavement racing, 13, 17, 18, 19, *42,* 43, *45,* 48
Pearson, Larry, *54, 55*
Pennsboro (W VA) Motor Speedway, 18, *19*
Petro, Russ, *63*
Petty, Kyle, *54, 55*
Petty, Richard, *11,* 11, 20, *20,* 22, *25, 34-5, 50-1, 52,* 68
pits, 22, 26, *27,* 30, *30, 31,* 68, *70-1, 72;* crews, 20, *20,* 22, *23, 24, 26,* 26, *27, 27,* 29, 30, 31, *31, 70-1*
Pocono Speedway, 54
Pontiac, 37, *46-7;* Firebird, 12; Purolator, *20-1,* STP, *20,* 35
Purvis, Larry, *77*

Rayburn, C J, *62, 62-3*
Reynolds, Burt, *76*
Robbins, Marty, *13*
Rudd, Ricky, *15, 33, 58-9*
Rush, Lonny Jr, *19, 41*
Ruttman, Troy, 12

Sauter, Jay, *19*
Schrader, Ken, *36, 55*
Shady Bowl Speedway, DeGraff, OH, *16, 42, 76*
Short Track Racing Stars (STARS), 13
short track racing, *16,* 17, *17,* 18, *19,* 31, *38,* 39, 48, 49, *49,* 53, 54, *56, 77*
Smith, Marvin, 68
street stocks, *33,* 34, 44, 45, *45*
superspeedways, 15, 17, 20, *22,* 37, 39, 68, *69,* 73

Talladega (AL) Speedway, *12-13,* 14, 17, 68, *73*
tires, *22, 26,* 26, 27, 30, *30, 31,* 34, 45, 46, 48
trailers, 32, *33*

Vallo, John, *42,* 53, 54, *77*
Van Zant, Randy, *42*

Wallace, Kenny, *37*
Wallace, Rusty, *9, 37, 55, 76*
Waltrip, Darrell, 11, *24, 33, 36, 78-9*
Waltrip, Michael, *35*
Wilson, Wardell, *36*
Winchester (IN) Motor Speedway, *19, 43,* 44, *57*
Winston Cup, *1,* 11, 22, *25,* 26, *36, 37, 38, 56-7, 58-9,* 73, *73, 74-5, 76, 77;* cars, 34, 35, 36, 37, *39,* 39; West Series, 12
Wood Brothers, 31
World 100, 13, *64-5, 66-7, 76, 77*
World of Outlaws sprint car organization, 13

Young, Kim *44, 76*